Six Conversations

Six Conversations

A Simple Guide for Managerial Success

Steve King

Six Conversations
A Simple Guide for Managerial Success

iUniverse books may be ordered through booksellers or by contacting:

iUniverse
1663 Liberty Drive
Bloomington, IN 47403
www.iuniverse.com
1-800-Authors (1-800-288-4677)

ISBN: 978-1-4917-5817-5 (sc)
ISBN: 978-1-4917-5816-8 (e)

Library of Congress Control Number: 2015900521

Print information available on the last page.

iUniverse rev. date: 04/30/2015

Contents

For the Hewitt HR team ... whose patience and collaboration made the six conversations possible.

Chapter 1

Introduction

Why I Wrote this Book

Miles Davis, the great jazz trumpet player, reportedly once said that he never really played anything that had not already been played by Louis Armstrong. It was a grand compliment to an innovator who helped define jazz as a musical art form and the trumpet as one of the principle tools of that art form.

For any of us who choose to consult, speak, and teach about management, our Louis Armstrong is Peter Drucker. Most of us simply riff on Drucker's research and writings. A few years back, I ran across this quote from Drucker's classic 1954 book, *The Practice of Management.*

> "A manager develops people. Through the way he manages he makes it easy or difficult for them to develop themselves. He directs people or he misdirects them. He brings out what is in them or he

stifles them. He strengthens their integrity or he corrupts them. He trains them to stand upright and strong or he deforms them.

Every manager does these things when he manages—whether he knows it or not. He may do them well or he may do them wretchedly. But he always does them."

> "... good management of people, like a solid market strategy and selling products or services customers want, is an essential ingredient in the success of any business enterprise."

Strong words. I often start off management programs I facilitate with this quote to drive home the notion that the management of others is serious business. There is an old adage that says people do not leave their jobs or their companies; most of the time people leave their managers. Drucker's quote certainly lends credence to this adage.

I think the adage is probably a half-truth, but in this case half is a lot. People leave their jobs for plenty of reasons. Some of those reasons, such as leaving a job for another job with better insurance coverage, managers really have no influence over at all. Other reasons, however, like someone's desire to learn new skills or pursue new career opportunities, can be impacted quite a bit by the quality of your manager.

This book is about the latter, the half of a manager's role that makes employees more productive and engaged with their work. Or, as Drucker might say, the half that brings out the best in employees, strengthens their integrity, and trains them to stand upright and strong.

I have written it because I believe that good management of people, like a solid market strategy and selling products or services that customers want, is an essential ingredient in the success of any business enterprise. I have written this book because I want to offer a few simple suggestions to help managers be good and sometimes great managers.

Good Conversations

I personally came to a management role late in my career. I was nearly forty when there was a restructuring of the learning and development group I was part of and I was tapped to manage three people who, up until that time, had been my peers. I have heard plenty of horror stories about this particular scenario of suddenly being the boss of those who were your peers the day before. Luckily for me, my transition went reasonably well. That was not because I was a natural-born manager; rather I credit my new staff and old friends with being professional, patient, and forgiving.

Interestingly, even though I had not managed folks before this assignment, I had taught supervisory programs to managers for a few years prior to becoming a manager. These were canned programs created by vendors and purchased by my company for some internal person (in this case, me) to deliver. Looking back on this arrangement—someone who had not managed teaching managers how to manage—it seems a little peculiar. But these programs were well designed, the content was good, and my teaching skills were adequate, so it worked.

Actually, I think it worked for an additional reason. Knowing that I would likely lack credibility teaching management skills when I had never been a manager, I began every class by acknowledging this fact but offering an alternative value proposition for my role in front of the group. I suggested that as someone who had been managed by others for years, I had insight into what good management was. And it was from that perspective that I taught managerial skills and techniques. In fact, I encouraged the participants to use the same frame of reference and approach the class from an "I am walking in my staff's shoes" point of view. And it worked. Participants seemed to more easily grasp management concepts, principles, and processes when viewing them from the other side of the desk even though the vendor materials were presented from the point of view of a manager.

Now I will admit that this notion of teaching basic management from the point of view of an employee started as an aid to accommodate my lack of managerial experience. But what I quickly figured out was this perspective was a more effective way of engaging new managers in building their managerial muscle since they could relate more readily to "being managed" than "managing."

I continued to teach frontline or supervisory management programs after I became a manager. But I did not abandon the notion that these kinds of classes should be facilitated from the point of view of employees. Instead I simply integrated my new experiences as a manager into my "in their shoes" angle on course materials.

It was during those first few years as both manager and instructor when I began to realize that employee expectations of their managers were really not that complicated after all. And a few years later, when I was given the responsibility of creating a performance management system for the company I worked for, I decided to use that opportunity to synthesize my thinking about employee needs and create an employee-centric approach to managing performance.

The result of that synthesis was "The Six Conversations." This book is about those six conversations—what they are; why they are important to the performance of employees, managers, and the whole organization; and how we effectively have these conversations.

Any manager reading this book has been either blessed or cursed by a performance management system that requires written goals, documented development plans, and performance ratings; compensation rationalization; assessments of flight risks; high-potential designations, and so on. I have been personally responsible for these systems in two large organizations and know both the value they can have and the burden they can create for managers.

This book is not a critique of these systems. Instead it is a simple suggestion. The suggestion is to first have good conversations with the folks who report to you about things that matter to them and things that matter to the business. Once managers have had these conversations, feed the performance management system with the output of those conversations. Don't let the performance process drive the conversations. Let the conversations drive the performance process.

So if you enjoy a good conversation ... read on.

Six Conversations

It turns out that employee expectations of managers are pretty simple. They want to be treated with respect. They want to be treated fairly.

"If a manager can successfully answer these six questions with their employees those employees will be productive and engaged at work."

Respect and fairness are sort of the table stakes a manager must ante up when he or she starts supervising others. While I will comment about respect and fairness off and on in this book, they are not the central focus.

Beyond respect and fairness, there are six questions most employees want their managers to help them answer. These questions are as follows:

1. What's expected of me?
2. What and how should I develop?
3. How am I doing?
4. How did I do?
5. How will I be rewarded?
6. What's next for me?

This book is based on following this simple proposition. If a manager can successfully answer these six questions with his or her employees (and treat employees with respect and fairness), those employees will be productive and engaged at work.

Here is how it can look:

Imagine each year beginning with a good conversation with your manager about what lies ahead for the business and the part you will play in the success of that business. Then a week or two later, another conversation focuses on skills you will develop during the year to ensure your performance continues to improve. As the months roll by, your manager has regular check-ins with you to make sure your performance and development are on track and offers some advice to keep things on track. Then maybe midyear you and your manager have a conversation about your career—where you might like to head in the company and what it would take to get there. Near the end of the year, your manager sits down to review your work and offers an assessment of how things went for you. And a couple of weeks later, your manager talks with you in an honest, open way about your salary and bonus if you are eligible.

Notice that in this description there are no forms being filled out or data being entered into a system. There are no dual signatures on documents or a human resources (HR) person in sight. There are simply conversations between the manager and his or her employee.

Not that there aren't forms to fill out or data to be entered into a system. Of course there probably are. But that documentation should be a by-product of good conversations. Documentation does not optimize individual productivity as much as excellent management does by facilitating good interactions with employees.

I don't want to oversell these six conversations. I do not think that these conversations along with some respect and fairness will get the whole management job done. There are other responsibilities, such as looking after work processes, attending to regulatory requirements, meeting management, and so on, that impact manager success as well. But I do think attending to these six conversations gets a great deal of the job done. And when someone is taking on his or her first role as a manager of people, I firmly believe arming the individual with this six-conversations framework, along with the skills and insights to have those conversations, sets these new managers and their staffs up for success.

So why not seven or eight conversations? Why six? The answer is threefold. First, it's best not to overload new managers, or anyone taking on a new role, with too many tasks at once. Six tasks turns out to be a manageable number. Second, the conversations are simply a response to the most-often-asked questions of managers by the people who work for them. If you doubt this, complete your own survey of employees and ask them what they want from their managers. I have many times, and these six reappear time and time again. And finally, the six conversations align nicely with typical components of a performance management system:

- Performance planning—What's expected of me?
- Development planning—What and how should I develop?
- Feedback—How am I doing?
- Performance assessment—How did I do?
- Compensation management—How will I be rewarded?
- Career management—What's next for me?

As I said earlier, conversations first and then process. But it is wise to align the conversations with these inevitable and necessary processes.

Let's look at each of the six, one at a time.

Chapter 2

What's Expected of Me?

Employees ask the "What's expected of me?" question to understand what work they need to get done and what they will be rewarded for. It is basically a goal-setting conversation.

Good goals for individuals in a workplace have certain characteristics. Often the acronym SMART is used to describe those characteristics. SMART stands for specific, measurable, attainable, relevant, and timely. I will return to SMART in a moment.

What do employees want out of a "What's expected of me?" conversation? Most want clear goals that are fair and maybe even developmental. Fair in this case means "doable." Most employees don't mind a little stretch in some of their goals. In fact, those staff members most interested in developing and growing their skills understand that some stretch in their performance goals is the way to grow their talents.

One way to ensure that sense of fairness is to include the employees in creating their own performance goals. Managers are accountable for making sure performance goals exist for each of their employees, so the final say on the goals needs to be the manager's. But I think a good practice is for a manager to write up a preliminary set of goals, share those goals as a draft with each staff member, and then discuss those goals together until a final version is reached. In most cases this collaborative approach to creating goals creates a higher level of commitment than if the goals were presented to the employee as a done deal.

What do managers and their bosses want from the "What's expected of me?" conversation? Employees committed to their goals—yes. But management's

> "In order for a manager to have an effective "What's expected of me?" conversation, they must first understand the business objectives ..."

interest is in making sure employee goals link to the objectives of the business. In a fast-food restaurant, the business objective is to make money by serving customers low-cost meals that can be prepared and serviced quickly and pleasantly. So typical expectations of the folks manning the counter are to efficiently and accurately take and place the customer's order, collect the money, and distribute the food—all with a smile. The employee's goals are tied to the business goals.

In order for managers to have an effective "What's expected of me?" conversation, they must first understand the business objectives and then translate those objectives into goals for their employees.

Typical business objectives are:

- revenue, expense, and margin targets
- productivity targets
- customer satisfaction targets
- employee engagement and retention targets
- sustainability goals
- meeting regulatory requirements

The expectations mentioned a moment ago for counter workers would be primarily productivity and customer satisfaction related business objectives.

Some companies do a great job clarifying business objectives that can be used to help organize employee goals. I worked for a company that published what it called "the six pack," which consisted of six business goal categories to which every employee had to tie their own goals. In that particular case, the categories were financial, customer, team, compliance, quality, and operational excellence. Each category had company- and unit-wide goals associated with it. Managers and employees simply wrote their goals accordingly.

Employee goals tend to be (1) singularly results oriented or (2) results plus process oriented. Results-oriented goals state the desired outcome and leave it to the employee to decide how to achieve it—usually within some understood guidelines. For example, a salesperson might have a goal to sell one thousand units every month. A "results plus process"-oriented goal is more prescriptive, suggesting not only the outcome but also the way in which the work must be done. For example, a salesperson might have a goal to sell one thousand units every month using a particular sales process and set of tools.

I have found that which type of goal you choose—results only or results plus process—depends on such factors as the culture of the company, the risk associated with not following a prescribed process, the complexity of the work, or the newness of the employee. Some employees like to be told exactly what to do; others don't. A manager's job is to size up the need for following particular processes and work out goals accordingly. But as a general rule of thumb, if there is that need, write it into the goal. If there is not, clarify the outcome and empower employees to get it done as they see fit.

All of this—employee input, reflection on business goals, the nature of employee goals—is fodder for the "What's expected of me?" conversation.

How SMART Should You Be?

So goals should be fair, tied to the business, and appropriately focused on either a result or a result and an associated process. Conventional wisdom also says they should be SMART. Here is a quick decoding of the acronym.

- Specific—What am I responsible for?
- Measurable—How will I be measured?
- Attainable—Do I have the capability and resources I need?
- Relevant—How does this meet a business need, fit with my role, and help my development?
- Timely—What is my deadline?

The wisdom is that goals should be written as if to answer all of those questions. Here are two examples of weakly written goals improved by applying SMART principles.

- From: Recruit five new salespeople.
- To: Recruit five new sales reps for the Midwest region with at least ten years of pharmaceutical sales experience. Have these new sales reps on board in the first ninety days of the new fiscal year in order to positively impact Q4 sales forecast.
- From: Redesign delivery routes.
- To: Redesign the delivery routes in a fashion that saves 10 percent fuel consumption without extending driver workdays. Have these new routes operational by May 1. Allowing for some adjustments to the routes with experience, have fuel consumption target hit by September.

It is hard to argue against SMART goals. They bring clarity to work expectations, improve the chances that related business goals are met, and make end-of-the-year assessment (how did I do?) easier. So why is it that you so rarely see performance

"It is hard to argue against SMART goals."

goals actually written like the two examples above? Why is it so many people know SMART and so few people actually use it?

I think there are a handful of reasons. First, it is harder and requires more work and more thinking to get done. Second, it feels to some like micromanaging or maybe even a little insulting in its detail. Third, our work environments regularly change, and the details of SMART goals often need updating when changes occur—so why bother? Finally, sometimes employees and even their managers don't want to make such clear commitments. It's better and less risky to error on the side of ambiguity.

I don't have much time for numbers one, two, and four. I think they are bogus excuses. Most of the time I think SMART goals are good. But I have some sympathy for number three in that list. When I know the world is on shifting sands, I will admit to having kept goals less SMART, figuring a "directional goal" can get someone started and details can be worked out later when things are a little clearer. This generally worked out for my employees and me.

It is easy to say that SMART is the guideline for writing or documenting goals, which is true. But I think the conversation prior to finalizing goals in a performance management system needs to be SMART as well. In fact, during the "What's expected of me?" conversation all SMART questions are sorted out and answered to both the manager's and the employee's satisfaction. Once that is done, it is time to document.

So my advice: despite the hassle and maybe the awkwardness of SMART goals, get in the habit of using them in your "What's expected of me?" conversations and then translate the content of those conversations into written goals.

Stretch Goals

One final thought about setting expectations and goals. To improve productivity and build in room for someone to professionally grow and develop, some goals should be "stretch" goals. By stretch goals I mean goals that have just the right amount of risk that they will require the application of some new skill or knowledge, the use of a new tool or process, and perhaps a little extra effort.

I am not talking about unreasonable risk where the only way the goal can be reached is by luck or unfair expectations of effort. I am talking about just enough risk that the goal will be in jeopardy unless a little something extra is added. A good metaphor might be how we often think of Olympic athletes. You never hear Olympians competing in a track event like the mile run say they are going to shave thirty seconds off their time. It is unrealistic. Instead they talk in terms a shaving a second or two off their time. It becomes their stretch goal.

The following chart represents this notion of stretch goals well. The objective when discussing potential goals with a staff member is to make sure those goals fall in the fat part of the bell-shaped curve. Okay, maybe a couple of goals can be slam dunks. But the best performers will want most of their goals to stretch them, giving them the opportunity to develop and grow professionally. They will be motivated by the challenge.

Of course, there are always going to be a few people who want to load up on goals easily achieved. But I am not sure these folks are going to help you improve productivity and create capacity for business growth.

Motivation/Performance

Greatest motivation and performance

Too easy

Challenging

Too hard

Goal difficulty

"Managers should encourage a little risk taking and reassure their employee that resources will be made available to manage that risk"

In the "What's expected of me?" conversation, a manager and his or her staff member can sort out what the appropriate amount of stretch is for each goal. Managers should encourage a little risk taking and reassure their employees that resources will be made available to manage that risk—one key resource being opportunities to acquire new skills and knowledge. This reassuring moment in the "What's expected of me?" conversation is actually the gateway to our second conversation, "How or what should I develop?"

Example of a "What's Expected of Me?" Conversation

As we move through this book, I want to provide you with a glimpse into what each conversation looks like when done well. I am truncating or abridging my examples to highlight the essence of the conversations. The real conversations would be longer.

In each example you'll recognize me in the role of employee. The manager is Nancy, a fictitious amalgamation of many of my former managers and role models I keep in my thoughts when I try to manage well.

Nancy: Time for us to set some goals for next year, Steve. I want to focus on three areas. I want you to take the lead on the development of the new executive leadership program. I also want you to oversee the addition of some new modules for our supervisory program. Third, I have been asked if you could consult with the team looking at some process improvements for the bank's credit process. I want you to focus on those three goals. Do you have anything else you were expecting to be on your plate?

Steve: I was kind of hoping I would get the chance to help with the revamping of the cash management curriculum since I have not worked with that group much.

Nancy: Okay. Let's talk about that as well. Let's start with the executive program. We intend to select a university provider to partner with us on this. The C-suite wants a regional university, so you already know the list of likely partners. We are looking to spend roughly two hundred thousand per year on this program and run twenty high potentials per year through it over the next five years. They want the first program to run in the fall.

Steve: The numbers seem reasonable. I've selected and worked with plenty of vendors but never a university. I might need a little help there.

Nancy: Leslie has developed programs with universities before so she can give you some guidance.

Steve: Okay. Are the program objectives anywhere beyond conceptual yet?

Nancy: The C-suite has already brainstormed what they hope will be covered in the program. They are really into this, and I think the commitment level to get it done is high. But you know that once we start talking with universities, they are going to bring some new thoughts to the party. Somewhere between selecting the external partner and finishing off the design overview or blueprint for C-suite endorsement we'll have to set the objectives in concrete. Is that a problem?

Steve: No, I think I could make that work.

Nancy: We need the selection done by April first and a design blueprint for the program signed off on by June thirtieth. CEO would like the program to run in the fall.

Steve: Fall should not be a problem. And I expect April first is not a problem for selection, that is, if Leslie can help me get up to speed on academic speak. But you know how development work goes. In the best of circumstances, we can barely create full programs based on an agreed-upon design in three months. And with such a high-profile program and each member of the C-suite likely to want to place their fingerprints on this, three months is probably not realistic.

Nancy: But fall is?

Steve: Yes, I think so, if you give me Ronnis and Russ to help with the development. If I have those two working with me say about twenty-five percent of their time after April first, we can shorten the development time and still hit fall. October thirty-first, right? Not September fifteenth?

Nancy: Okay, yes. I think I can sell that.

Steve: So the goal is to deliver an executive development program to twenty of our high potentials by October thirty-first using a regional university as our partner. Leslie helps me with navigating the new academic waters, and Russ and Ronnis are made available to me half time from April until November.

Nancy: Yes. We good?

Steve: Yes. Now, what do you have in mind for the supervisory program?

Commentary on the Conversation

I wrote this conversation as an example of how it would look if it goes pretty well. Unfortunately not all conversations go so smoothly. So let's imagine challenges Nancy could have encountered in the conversation.

In this case Steve seemed to have a pretty good idea of what it would take to realistically develop a program with tight time frames, and he was ready to negotiate for the resources he needed. Nancy concurred, so the negotiation was quite easy. But what if Nancy felt she could not give Steve extra resources?

Steve: But you know how development work goes. In the best of circumstances we can barely create full programs based on an agreed-upon design in three months. And with such a high-profile program and each member of the C-suite likely to want to place their fingerprints on this, three months is probably not realistic.

Nancy: But fall is?

Steve: Yes, I think so, if you give me Ronnis and Russ to help with the development. If I have those two working with me say about twenty-five percent of their time after April first, we can shorten the development time and still hit fall. October thirty-first, right? Not September fifteenth?

Nancy: Ronnis and Russ are not an option. They already have plenty on their plates.

Steve: I'll need someone else then. Maybe you can hire a contractor to work with me?

Nancy: Why do you think you can't handle it yourself?

Steve: I haven't worked with the C-suite that much, but my impression is that they will push their differing perspectives on how the program should look, and I will be stuck trying to reconcile what is not reconcilable.

Steve is resisting taking on the work solo. Nancy thinks he can and should handle it alone. She could have simply said no to his request for help and moved on. The risk in that approach is she might leave Steve feeling unheard and set up to fail. Or she could have given in to the request, despite her better judgment, and allowed valuable resources (Ronnis and Russ) to be reassigned work, probably leaving a resource hole somewhere else. Nancy's question "Why do you think you can't handle it yourself?" is the best response. It allows her to hear what really underlies Steve's request for resources and help. In this case we find out a lack of experience with the C-suite and some assumptions about the C-suite's behavior are at the heart of his concerns. By the way, Nancy might have to probe around a little to get Steve to admit to these assumptions. He may not be able to articulate those concerns readily. But the key is that she recognized Steve's resistance and probed to understand. This is good management.

Once the concerns are in the open and discussed, Nancy has options. She can agree with Steve and give him the resources. Or she can disagree with Steve and insist he handle it on his own. If she goes with the latter, she should explain why she thinks he can handle it. She might shed some light on C-suite behavior. She might share examples in which Steve has been successful with tight time frames before. She might suggest that while she cannot provide Ronnis and Russ 25 percent of the time, getting their perspectives over lunch or coffee is still available for Steve. She might even suggest this is a developmental opportunity for Steve.

Maybe these perspectives persuade Steve, or maybe they don't. As the manager, Nancy has the final say on what is expected of him. Being authentic with Steve in this conversation is the key. She should listen carefully to his perspectives. She should share her perspectives. Once fact, experiences, and assumptions are shared and discussed, Nancy should make the final call. In this case the revised SMART goal sounds like this:

> Deliver an executive development program to twenty of our high potentials by October 31, using a regional university as partner. Leslie can help with navigating the new academic waters, and Steve can informally tap Russ and Ronnis for advice on the development of the course.

Steve may not be completely satisfied with this conclusion, but at least he had a fair hearing of his concerns. Sometimes this is the best outcome a manager can hope for.

Chapter 3

What and How Should I Develop?

Many research papers, like Towers Watson's "Global Trends in Employee Attraction, Retention,

"It has always baffled me why managers ignore development."

and Engagement" (October 2014), for example, explore why people leave their jobs for other jobs. As you can imagine, there are plenty of reasons for changing roles, even changing companies. Most rank the desire to develop and gain new skills as one of the primary reasons people move on. These findings would be consistent with the work of those who study why people work. Their conclusions suggest there are quite a few of us who have the intrinsic need to master our chosen professions—beyond just being proficient.

The actions of managers influence decisions of others to stay or to go. This is because managers can encourage the development of their people, ignore it, or sometimes even discourage it. It has always baffled me why managers ignore development. Skilled workers are more productive, more engaged, and remain longer within their roles, in their units, and with their companies. It seems simply like good business to develop your staff.

So it is no wonder the folks who work for us often ask, "What and how should I develop?"

Let me acknowledge before I go any further that while I am baffled by managers who would ignore the development of their folks, I am not baffled by managers putting it off. Sometimes our daily routines conspire against us getting to our own development and the development of others. There is an old story I have heard repeated now and again that explains how this can happen.

There was a lumberjack who cut down an average of twenty-five trees each day. One day a brand-new ax, shiny and sharp, arrived in the mail. The first day he used the new ax he cut down thirty trees and declared what a fine ax it was. Over the next couple of days, his productivity remained thirty downed trees per day.

On the fourth day, he cut down twenty-eight trees, and on the fifth day he cut down twenty-five. Disturbed, he made the commitment that he would work harder on day six and down thirty trees once again. And he did, but he worked an extra hour to get it done. The next day he cut down only twenty-five trees and the following day just twenty-three trees.

There he sat at end of the day, unhappy about his own lack of productivity and committing without enthusiasm to working harder.

A buddy wandered by and noticed the lumberjack was down and out. When his friend heard the predicament, he suggested the lumberjack simply sharpen his ax. The lumberjack exclaimed, "I can't do that! I don't have time to do that! I just have to work harder!"

Of course, the moral of this story is that sometimes we need to take a little time and sharpen our axes—sharpening being a metaphor for training and the myriad of other ways people can learn new things. Managers have to provide others with the opportunity to sharpen their axes.

So how do people learn new skills? For example, how can a new project manager learn to become a good project manager?

One easy way to think about how to develop someone is to apply what's sometimes called the 70/20/10 rule. This rule suggests that roughly 70 percent of what we learn, we learn "on the job." This means that we learn while we are doing the work, sometimes under the watchful eye of an expert and sometimes by unguided trial and error. So a new project manager learns by managing ever-increasingly difficult projects, picking up what works and what does not work as they move along. While it sounds kind of inefficient, in fact it is quite an effective way to learn since it is "learning by doing."

The twenty of the 70/20/10 rule suggests that 20 percent of what we learn we learn through direct feedback from others—maybe a formal coach or mentor, maybe informal feedback from a peer or client. In the case of new project managers, they might get assigned a mentor who meets with them once a month to discuss what's worked, what hasn't worked, and what can be learned from those experiences.

The ten of the 70/20/10 rule suggests that 10 percent of what we learn we learn from formal training programs. In the case of new project managers, they might be sent to a project-management training program or asked to review an online course on project management.

So a new project manager's development plan might look like this:

1.   Start and complete project X.

2. Meet with your manager each week to review not only the progress of the project but also what was learned that could be applied to future projects.

3. Meet with an assigned project coach (expert) to ask for advice as new, unfamiliar things pop up while the project is being carried out.

4. Sign up and complete a three-day project management course before starting the project to get a sense of common tools, techniques, and best practices.

The 70/20/10 rule is a simple way for managers to think about the "how." What about the "what"? How can a manager pinpoint what a staff member's developmental needs are?

Determining Developmental Needs

When a manager and an employee sit down to talk about the employee's developmental needs, there are two perspectives that should shape that conversation. The first has to do with the skills and knowledge required to do the current job. The second is about the skills and knowledge required to do a future job.

Let's start with the perspective of the current job. If the "What's expected of me?" conversation has been handled

> "It is in these stretch goals that the clues for developmental needs can be found."

and documented well, someone who works for you should have a list of performance goals, some of which are stretch goals. It is in these stretch goals that the clues for developmental needs can be found. Most of the time the stretch in a stretch goal is tied to the developmental need. Here are three examples:

1. Deb has a performance goal that reads "Conduct a behavior-based 360 assessment of the firm's five senior leaders, provide each leader with feedback personally, and help each leader create an action plan for improving key behaviors. Complete the assessment, report, and create an action plan by March 1." In this case, Deb has administered 360 assessments before, but she has never been the person to report back to executives on their results and to help create action plans. So reporting and action planning are the developmental needs Deb might focus on.

2. Mark has a performance goal that reads "Sell the new upgraded version of the payroll system to five new or existing clients in the third and fourth quarters of this fiscal year." In this case, Mark has been quite successful at selling the earlier versions of the payroll systems. So his developmental need will be to learn about the upgrades and prepare to use that knowledge in his sales pitch.

3. Tara has a performance goal that reads "Manage the move of one hundred people and all related office equipment and technologies to a new office location by June 30 at a cost of under $500,000." In this case, Tara has never managed such a move or managed such a big project. So she will need plenty of development ranging from project management training to things like working with moving professionals, IT professionals, and real estate professionals. And since any move of people is laced with people issues, a good dose of change management knowledge would be in order.

Mark's developmental needs are probably the easiest to address. Maybe just a little one-on-one time with a product specialist (coaching and feedback—the 20 percent) and a trial run with a potential client (on-the-job learning—the 70 percent) will do the trick.

Tara certainly has the largest developmental challenge in front of her. If there was time, a crash course in project management and change management (training—the 10 percent], some regular time with real estate and IT folks (coaching and feedback—the 20 percent), and lots of "just doing and adjusting" (on-the-job learning—the 70 percent] would all be in order.

These examples focus on when a new stretch goal is established and development is needed to address the stretch. Occasionally someone has been working hard on a particular goal for a while and is just falling short of expectations. When that happens, a manager considers the many reasons for weak performance. It might be a lack of skills or knowledge, suggesting a training solution. There might be other reasons, such as the employee lacks motivation to attend to the work, or the employee has not been given the proper technology or machinery to attend to the work. Setting those other reasons aside for the moment, if development to improve poor performance is required, the same analysis and action plan can be used. If, in our example above, Deb had already started coaching senior executives and was struggling, a 70/20/10 development plan could be constructed and implemented.

I expect that most development plans will be focused on immediate and present performance needs. But someone's development plan might also include one or two development goals that are focused on future roles and responsibilities. Later in this book, we'll consider the "What's next for me?" conversation and, out of that conversation, suggestions for developmental needs that might best be started in advance of taking on the new role. Let's consider two examples here, and we'll revisit this notion of development for future roles in more detail later.

1. Frank is a successful salesperson with many of the qualities the company feels would make him a great manager of people. Within a year, a key regional sales manager role is expected to open up due to a retirement. Frank is deemed the likely successor for that role. So his development plan might include taking a sales management class and spending some one-on-one time with the current regional manager before that manager retires, learning the ropes, so to speak. This would be leveraging the training/10 percent and coaching/20 percent strategies of development for a future role.

2. Sophie is a cook apprenticing with a master chef. Sophie is ambitious and hopes to become an executive chef in the next five or six years. Her development plan might include two or three moves from one restaurant and master chef to another. This would be leveraging the on-the-job learning/70 percent strategy of development for a future role.

It is worth pointing out that Frank and Sophie represent two slightly different developmental circumstances. In Frank's case, his future move is jointly negotiated between Frank and the company that views him in a new future role and is acting on that point of view in advance. In Sophie's case, she is plotting her own career course and the related development plan. Sophie's bosses might be encouraging her to pursue her dream and helping with those moves from restaurant to restaurant. Or they may not be. Either way, Sophie is more singularly in charge of her development plan around a future, desired role.

On occasion a manager might encounter someone with no interest in development at all. This could happen if an employee has no stretch goals and has no ambitions beyond the current role he or she is in. Is that okay? Probably not.

Some people simply love their jobs and want to stay in them. Think about grade school teachers. Some of them teach the same grade year in and year out. If they are good at it, parents tend to like this. Their son may have this teacher one year, and a couple of years later his sister has that same teacher; the parents are delighted. There's nothing wrong with someone liking his or her job and wanting to stay in it.

Having no stretch goals, on the other hand, is problematic. First, it suggests no change happens that will require new skills or new knowledge. Second, it suggests no change in productivity is expected because there is no acquisition of a new skill or new knowledge. Honestly, in today's economy it is hard to imagine a job that never changes or that a job's management would not expect more productivity from year after year.

So we can expect to rarely find a circumstance where someone would not need a development plan.

Example of a "What and How Should I Develop?" Conversation

Nancy: Steve, a couple of weeks ago we talked about you working on the new trust operations development program. Have you talked with George and some of his folks in trust about the need and expectations?

Steve: Yes. Honestly it seems pretty straightforward. The program will be for a new cohort of trainees each year. We'll simply plug in the American Bankers Association modules on the trust business and trust operations at the front end when the trainees arrive. Then each trainee will be assigned to a different role in ops for about two months. There are essentially six roles so the full rotation will take a year. Since the trainees all begin on the same day and they can be taking the ABA classes while they are rotating through jobs, the whole experience can be done in a year.

Nancy: So any concerns?

Steve: For me? Only one. George wants a test administered at the end of each ABA module. You know, sort of proof that each trainee knows what he or she is supposed to know. He wants to use any deficiencies that arise from the tests addressed during the rotations on the job. I honestly don't think this is a bad idea. In fact, it's kind of clever.

Nancy: What's the problem?

Steve: The ABA modules don't come with tests. I have never constructed a serious pencil-and-paper test before. Taken them all my life, but never built one. I am sure I can slap one together. But if we are going to do this, I want to do it right and make sure the test is a valid reflection of what is being taught in those modules.

Nancy: Interesting. Now that I think about it, I have never had to put together a serious test on some technical banking subject either. Any ideas?

Steve: I found a decent-looking book on test construction. I think I'd start there and get the basics. Looks like a quick read.

Nancy: Our compliance training has testing at the end of each module. Our legal folks put that training together with some help from an outside vendor. I think the vendor is local. Let's see if we can hook you up with the vendor for some advice and counsel on writing tests. Maybe you can even arrange to show them some first drafts and get their insights on how to improve those drafts. Use them as mentors of sorts.

Steve: I like that. I don't think I am on a huge learning curve here. Reading the book on basic test construction techniques and getting some advice from someone who has done this before should be enough. I just don't think I should take it on cold, so to speak.

Nancy: Agreed. Give legal a call today. Since this all begins in two months, you have some time. But have all of your ducks in a row—the book read and a mentor lined up—within a month.

Commentary on the Conversation

Note that all three parts of the 70/20/10 rule are in play here. The book is the formal learning. Those who will advise Steve on test construction are mentoring. And using each test in the program provides on-the-job trial-and-error instruction.

Also worth noting is that the emerging development plan has some of the same characteristics as a SMART performance goal. It could have easily been written like this:

- Be able to construct a valid test for each ABA trust module by learning appropriate test construction techniques prior to the start of the new trust operations development program.

In the conversation described on the previous page, things were handled casually. But in some cases the output from these development conversations needs to be formalized and documented. If that is the case, consider writing a development goal like a performance goal.

What if Steve proceeded with the trust work without identifying his lack of skills in test construction? What if he had built some tests that simply did not work? Then this development conversation would have had a more remedial ring to it and might have been more difficult.

Nancy: I spoke with George this week, and he is disappointed with the tests being used in the program. He doesn't think they assess knowledge of the ABA content seriously enough. In fact, he has had comments like that from a few of the trainees as well.

Steve: Their application of the content back on the job is the real test. If things are going well there, things are fine.

Nancy: That is not the point. We have committed to developing valid and reliable tests, and we are not meeting that expectation. Why is that? You still think the tests are a good idea?

Steve: Yes, I still think testing is a good idea. But I thought I was putting together some good tests.

Nancy: Have you run them by anyone with test construction experience?

Steve: No, not really.

Nancy: Have you constructed tests like these before?

Steve: No.

Nancy: And you really think the tests are a valuable part of the process?

Steve: Yes.

Nancy: I think you need to do some homework on test construction. What do you think?

Steve: Well, I have taken plenty of tests. I didn't think it would be that hard.

Nancy: But look at the outcome. Clearly something is not working here. I think you need to develop some skills here.

There is an old adage that says if someone is not doing something well, it is probably either a "will" issue or a "skill" issue. In this case you see Nancy ruling out the "will" issue with questions like "And you really think the tests are a valuable part of the process?" and then focusing on Steve's possible "skill" issue. Note that Nancy keeps tying the conversation back to Steve's performance and the client's unmet expectations, which is smart since it grounds the conversation in results and not process.

Chapter 4

How Am I Doing, and How Did I Do?

We are going to consider the "How am I doing?" and "How did I do?" conversations at the same time since both are essentially about feedback. "How am I doing?" focuses on giving someone feedback in the moment and is typically *developmental* in nature. This means that you as the manager are putting your coach hat on and offering up encouragement and advice on someone's performance and behavior. "How did I do?" is more of an *evaluation* conversation. This question is typically answered in a formal assessment setting, such as someone's annual performance review or a debriefing of performance after the completion of a project.

> "Perhaps one of the difficult moments in a manager/employee relationship is the performance review."

Let's start with the "How did I do?" conversation.

Perhaps one of the difficult moments in a manager/employee relationship is the performance review. When I have spoken to brand-new managers, many say performance reviews and managing conflict on the team often compete for the number one and number two least favorite things to do.

This is completely understandable. Performance assessments are about casting judgment, and most of us are uncomfortable judging others— particularly when we have to deliver negative feedback.

The difficulty is compounded because in most organizations performance ratings are given out during the performance review. Most of us have an awkward relationship with performance ratings. In school many of us are told that an "A" or "B" is good and anything else is merely average or worse. So if your company has a five-point evaluation scale—1,2,3,4,5 (with 5 being "great" and 1 being "not so great")—delivering any rating message other than a 4 or 5 can be hard.

And just to add a little more complexity to the mix, most organizations have a performance evaluation form that needs to be filled out and submitted to HR. These forms sometimes entice a manager to construct the "How did I do?" conversation around the form itself. Performance evaluation forms are built for documentation and justification for pay decisions, not conversations. So I have found form-driven conversations stilted and kind of cold. Forms have their place. I see value in documenting performance conversations. But the conversation itself is the key to good performance assessment, not the form.

Years ago I developed a framework for conducting performance reviews focused on having productive performance conversations. I call the framework Brag, Worry, Wonder, Bet. Here is how it works.

Think about someone you would like to give feedback to. For our purposes here, we'll call her Michelle. Before meeting with Michelle, outline your thoughts using these four statements:

- When I brag about Michelle, I brag about
  _____.

- When I worry about Michelle, I worry about
  _____.

- When I wonder about Michelle, I wonder about
  _____.

- If I were to bet on Michelle, I would bet on

  _____.

Each of these statements is designed to address specific issues and opportunities. In another book I have written, titled *Brag, Worry, Wonder, Bet*, I go into a great deal of detail about this framework and its use. Let me give you the most basic overview.

- Brags are about the things that are going well and that you want to reinforce.
- Worries are about the things that are not going well and that you want to address, improve, and remedy.
- Wonders are curiosities about things that may impact performance, but you are not sure.
- Bets are predictions of what could happen in the future.

These are four words that you do not usually find being used in the workplace. They are simple words, pedestrian words. It turns out that is part of what makes them powerful words.

Once a manager has gathered his or her thoughts using this framework, he or she should use the framework to actually have the conversation. After the conversation, the manager can turn his or her attention to completing the requisite forms. But first, the conversation.

Example of the "How Did I Do?" Conversation
Using Brag, Worry, Wonder, Bet

The easiest way to understand how "brag, worry, wonder, bet" is used
in a performance review is to see it in action. So here is an example
with some commentary afterward. Once again, what you will read is a
truncated version of a typical performance review. But in this case the
key concepts are being covered.

Nancy: Ready for your performance review?

Steve: Yes, let's go.

Nancy: I want to start with my brags about you. I have three key brags
about your performance this year. First, the trust operations
program was a big hit. The leaders in the trust department are
quite pleased. The trainee rotation process worked beautifully,
and the performance of those trainees exceeded expectations. I
know there will be a few tweaks for the next group. But all in
all, what a great outcome.

The second brag is your design of the new executive leadership
program. Nearly everyone in the pilot of the program raved
about the way you used the 360 feedback tool as the framework
for the course content. Since everyone had received a feedback
report before the program, they came primed with questions
and ready to improve. You did a great job creating motivation
for learning new leadership skills. More importantly, leaders are
clearly using their new skills back on the job. In fact, I saw the
CEO use one of the tactics taught in the program in a meeting
just the other day.

Steve: Thanks.

Nancy: And I want to make sure I tell you the two new modules for the
supervisory program are great. Our managers really needed

that change management module in particular, considering all the change happening around here. I thought it provided some real practical tools for managers and post course evaluations certainly validated that. We have plenty of folks signed up for future offerings, so the word has clearly gotten out there. The module on influence was good as well, but the change module was a home run.

In all three cases, you met the goals we set out in the performance plan for you this year. Well done.

Do you have anything to add? Other big brags on your radar this year?

Steve: No, I think those are the best pieces of my work this year. I think I learned the most from building the trust program. But it was all good.

Nancy: I have only one worry about your performance this year. It has to do with your consulting on credit process redesign. We have already talked about this a couple of times, but I need to bring it up once again. I am worried that you did not make enough time on your calendar for this project. The team members really needed your process improvement expertise, and often it looks like they were left on their own to figure things out. I don't think your inattention to the project impacted the quality of that team's efforts per se. But I do think it impacted how long it took the team to complete the work. They struggled without your guidance.

Steve: But Nancy, I had a lot on my plate this year. Something was going to drop.

Nancy: But this worries me.

Steve: Why?

Nancy: You are building a good reputation as a learning person here at the bank. But we need to expand your portfolio of skills. Look, if I were to bet on you, I would bet that in three or four years you could do my job. I really think you have the talent to do it. We can talk about this in a moment. But to advance in the bank you will need to build new skills and be seen as a more multidimensional player. The credit project was your chance to do that, and I worry that you missed your opportunity. That team sees your performance contribution as merely average, and that's a shame since I know you could have contributed more.

Steve: You think I messed up?

Nancy: I'm worried you missed an opportunity. If your plate was really that tight, we should have considered reprioritizing your plate. We talked about this during the year, but you said you had it under control. Now you're saying something dropping off your plate was inevitable. I am worried there was a breakdown in workload management here.

Steve: Okay. I see the point. I get it.

Nancy: I wonder if you were really interested in playing that role of process consultant to the credit team in the first place. Were you?

Steve: Yes, I was. I know it was a little different use of my skills and an opportunity to do something other than build and run training programs.

Nancy: I wonder why, when you were slammed for time, that you picked the training work rather than the consulting work. I wonder if it is because training is in your comfort zone and consulting is not.

Steve: I'll have to think about that, but you might be right.

Nancy: Let's pick up on that when we set your performance goals for next year. Maybe there is a stretch goal in there somewhere for you. Ideally I would like to see you continue to have some consulting work on your plate next year for your development.

Steve: Okay.

Nancy: So all in all it's been a good year for you, Steve. I will be giving you a performance rating of "meets expectations" despite the challenges on the credit process assignment. I think when I look at the whole year and all that's on your plate, this is a fair assessment.

Let me return to that bet I mentioned earlier. Honestly, Steve, if I were to bet on you, I would bet that you could do my job or a job like mine someday. It's not a long shot either. You'll need some more exposure to senior management, and you'll have to expand your skill sets to include consulting. But this is all doable.

Steve: If you had asked me two years ago, I would have said no, I am not interested in a role like yours. But now I am kind of interested.

We'll stop listening in on this conversation right here since it is drifting into a "What's next for me?" conversation. But let's take a moment and debrief this performance assessment.

Commentary on the Conversation

- The three brags were specific. There was an attempt in each case to highlight the impact of the work with such phrases as "trainee rotation process worked beautifully and the performance of those trainees exceeded expectations" and "leaders are clearly using their new skills back on the job. In fact, I saw the CEO use one of the tactics taught in the program in a meeting just the other day." And the brags were tied back to the performance goals. Brags should be specific, name impact, and link to performance goals.

- Likewise, the worry was specific, noting a failure to make impact and making a link to performance expectations. Note how Nancy used the word "worry." She set up the difficult feedback with the word. When Steve got defensive, she returned to the word twice more. With each use of the word, Steve got less defensive and began engaging in an authentic conversation. This is because the word "worry" carries a kind of emphatic tone that helps break down communication barriers between a manager and the person who works for the manager. "Worry" is not a magic word. I cannot guarantee that providing difficult feedback will always go well when you begin with that word. But my experience and the experience of others who have used this technique points to it working quite well most of the time. My suggestion is to try it out and see for yourself.

- Notice that Nancy used the word "wonder" to clarify Steve's original desire to do the credit project and whether Steve leaned into his comfort zone when he prioritized his work. This is a kind of organic use of the word "wonder," flowing from the worry portion of the conversation. Nancy can be a better manager when she knows with more certainty answers to these questions rather than making assumptions about them. A more formal use of the word "wonder" might have sounded something like "Steve, when I wonder about you, I wonder if you would like to eventually take on consulting as a full-time role and leave facilitation in the classroom behind for a while." This particular wonder statement could have satisfied some curiosity Nancy had about where Steve's interest in roles and responsibilities lies and then have been leveraged into a bet on Steve and his future.

- Nancy's bet was a career bet, which is the most typical way to use the word "bet." It is an excellent lead in to the "What's next for me?" conversation. Bets can also be used to suggest how much risk you think is associated with a task. That might sound like "I would like to see you take on more consulting work in the future, although I will have to admit that it is not a sure bet you will perform well at consulting right away."

As Nancy prepared for this "How did I do?" conversation, she followed some basic rules of thumb both in the preparation and the execution. Here is a simple checklist you can use to make certain you're delivering good performance assessments as well.

1. Work from prepared notes.
2. Stay focused on brags and worries tied to performance and development goals.
3. Ask them to expand on your comments (What else?).
4. Wonder about things during the review itself.
5. If there is a performance rating, tell them what it is.
6. Hold off on the rewards conversation for another time.
7. Telegraph but do not formalize new goals.
8. Have the career conversation (bets).

Brag, Worry, Wonder, Bet, and the "How Am I Doing?" Conversation

I want to make just a few comments about giving routine feedback. Most of us understand the importance of feedback in improving performance. It really does not matter what kind of endeavor we are involved in or how proficient we happen to be. Well-delivered and well-received feedback will almost always improve the quality of what we do.

Even the most successful athletes and musicians seek the advice of coaches and mentors to focus on mastering their performance. So why shouldn't we all do the same?

I once saw a simple model or equation that suggested the true importance of feedback. The equation looked like this:

$$performance = talent + effort + feedback$$

I like its simple message, suggesting that if someone has some innate talent, effort and feedback is what they need to build excellent performance. Presuming someone is working in a properly supportive environment—good tools, decent working conditions, reasonable processes, etc.—I think the equation is an accurate and powerful endorsement of the importance of feedback.

Can "brag, worry, wonder, bet" be used to give feedback on a regular basis to the folks who work with you, in addition to using it during performance reviews? The answer is yes.

It is as simple as integrating these words into routine conversations. Here are some examples:

- When you are in a team meeting, include an agenda item that requires each person on the team to brag about someone's recent performance, behavior, or display of a new skill.

- During a one-on-one with a staff member, indicate you are worried about some behavior you saw last week and you want to talk about it. Specifically use the word "worry," and if you are using that word in performance assessments, it will certainly catch the person's attention in a routine one-on-one.
- Set up flip charts in each corner of a room labeling each one with the words "brag, worry, wonder, bet," and ask members of your team to post notes on each flip chart indicating what they are bragging, worrying, wondering, and betting on. Give them five minutes to do this. Take down all the notes and discuss them as a team.
- Take a bunch of ideas pitched in an earlier brainstorming session and ask everyone to make a bet on which ideas are sure winners and which ideas are long shots.

Be creative in your use of the words. The objective would be to use those words often enough that they trigger a response that feedback is being delivered and someone should pay attention.

Chapter 5

Money and the "How Will I Be Rewarded?" Conversation

One of the most awkward conversations managers can have with their staff is the conversation about money. The "How will I be rewarded?" conversation is certainly about money. It is also about the intrinsic and intangible rewards a manager can offer his or her employees.

Let's start with the money. The research on how money motivates people is clear. People want to feel

> "People want to feel they are being treated "fairly" when it comes to pay."

they are being treated fairly when it comes to pay. Once that fairness "threshold" has been met, money is taken off the table, so to speak. Would people turn down more money, money above and beyond what they might think is fair? Probably not. But once staff members feel they are treated fairly, they tend to turn their attention to other types of workplace motivators, such as whether they are learning new skills or whether they have the work/life balance they want in their lives.

One of the things that can make a money conversation hard for a manager is the fact that managers typically only have marginal control over what they can pay people. In some companies HR sets the pay scales, and managers are given strict guidelines about the extent of base pay progression and bonus payout. In some businesses minimum wage defines what pay will be. In some companies pay is determined by a formula that links pay increases to business results. Some companies routinely only give cost-of-living increases. As long as all of these kinds of pay arrangements result in someone feeling he or she is being treated fairly, a manager will probably have an easier time with a pay conversation.

Your job as a manager is to deliver the pay message simply and with clarity. It might sound like this:

Nancy: Steve, I would like to review your new pay arrangements. This year you had a performance rating of "meets expectations." This warrants a 2.5 percent base increase this year. As you know you are also eligible for a twenty percent bonus. Based on the company's performance this year, we will be paying out bonuses at fifteen percent, just shy of the twenty percent. When we look at your pay compared to the market for roles like yours, we believe you are being paid around the market midpoint. Steve, we really appreciate both your efforts for the team and your impact on company. Do you have any questions?

Note a few things about this message. First, it is short and direct. Second, compensation is explicitly linked to performance—in this case both personal and company performance. Finally, market information is shared in this case in hopes that it telegraphs a sense of fairness.

What kinds of questions can typically come up after a message like this one is delivered? Some will be appropriate like "Where did the market data come from?" or "Why was the company performance below expectations this year?" Managers should give some thought to the kinds of questions they might get (often they are the same questions that they will have) and have some ready answers. Some questions may be inappropriate. For example, "Is my pay increase better than everyone else's?" or "Did everyone get the same bonus?" Talking about other people's pay distracts from the point and should be prohibited by policy. Again, think ahead of time about what inappropriate questions might be asked and determine how you will answer them.

Intrinsic Motivation and the "How Will I Be Rewarded?" Conversation

The word "reward" seems to imply money to most of us. But the truth is we are all rewarded by many other motivations at work as well. Managers often have a good deal more leeway to use some of these other motivators when they are trying to engage their staff. Here is a short, but not complete, list of things besides money that motivate people to do great work.

- development of new professional skills
- a good benefits package
- great facilities
- inspirational company goals
- good career opportunities
- pleasant coworkers
- flexible work arrangements

Like pay, most managers have little control over a company's benefits package, the quality of the facilities, or a company's mission and vision. If these kinds of things happen to be present in your workplace, the manager's job of motivating or rewarding becomes easier.

But there are things on this list, such as development, career, and team dynamics, that managers can significantly impact. The "What and how should I develop?" conversation is certainly an opportunity to motivate an employee to stay and do good work. In a moment, when we turn our attention to the "What's next for me?" conversation, we'll see it also is an opportunity to motivate an employee to stay and do good work. Providing employees some scheduling flexibility may or may not be a matter of policy in some companies. And in some businesses, flexibility is hard if customer requirements simply demand someone is present. But whenever a manager can shake loose some time, even for things like getting kids to school in the morning or attending to an elderly parent's health needs, this goes a long way in creating engagement with certain employees.

Over the last two decades there has been some very good research done on how people are motivated at work—particularly intrinsic or intangible kinds of motivation. If you are interested in digging deep into intrinsic motivation in the workplace, I would recommend reading either Daniel Pink's book *Drive* or Kenneth Thomas's book *Intrinsic Motivation at Work*. Pink's work suggests that if money is not an issue (fairness achieved), then autonomy at work, being able to master certain skills, and connecting to a higher sense of purpose are key to motivating folks in the workplace to stay and do great work. Thomas argues similarly that a sense of choice, a sense of meaningfulness, a sense of competency, and a sense of progress are key intrinsic motivators in the workplace.

It is important that managers see these intangible motivators as a kind of reward. Economists call these "psychic rewards." What would a "How will I be psychically rewarded?" conversation look like? It depends on what particular intrinsic motivators are important to a particular person. For me, a sense of choice or autonomy is very important. So any manager who explains that he or she will give me elbow room to achieve performance goals as I see fit is having a rewards conversation with me. If someone is motivated by a sense of purpose or meaningfulness, a conversation about how the individual's work links to the company's mission or vision or business strategy is probably a rewards conversation. If someone is motivated by mastery or a sense of competency, discussing regular coaching sessions designed to improve skills is probably a rewards conversation. And if someone is motivated by a sense of progress, setting and celebrating milestones along the way toward large performance goals is probably a form of the rewards conversation.

If you are in a situation where people generally feel they are not being paid fairly, I cannot lie to you; you are probably working (motivationally) against the current. But even if that is the case, focusing on intrinsic motivators can help win some employee engagement back and probably solidify a good relationship between you and your staff.

One last thought. Each one of us is motivated by different things. And these motivations are not static. They change over time. So as a manager it is smart to talk with each person who works for you and clarify what motivates him or her. This is also a "How will I be rewarded?" conversation. Take either Pink's or Thomas's framework or find a list of things that motivate you in the workplace and use it as a tool in the conversation. Determine what motivates your folks and use that to build a customized motivation plan for each. And check in on this every so often to make sure you're targeting the most current motivations, not last year's.

> "Each one of us are motivated by different things. And these motivations are not static. They change over time."

Chapter 6

What's Next for Me?

I worked at an organization that conducted a survey about how often these six conversations take place, and it found that the one conversation that took place the least was the "What's next for me?" conversation. When we unpacked why this was happening, we found a handful of reasons. Here are some of them:

- Managers worried that if they had a regular career conversation, they would be implying they were unhappy with someone or were encouraging someone to leave.
- Managers wanted to hoard the talent they had.
- Managers thought only one dimensionally about careers, meaning the only next job was their manager job. So if the manager was going nowhere, why bother to talk to others about their careers?
- Managers were not sure the company supported them having career conversations.

- Managers did not know about other opportunities in their companies and were therefore uncomfortable addressing the issue.
- Managers thought careers were the employees' responsibility and therefore they did not need to discuss it with them.

> "If managers sidestep this conversation, they can expect to be blindsided someday when their best performers serve notice that they are leaving for another job."

Each of these concerns is understandable, although something like "hoarding" talent is pretty selfish. The simple truth is most people are interested in advancing their career. If managers sidestep this conversation, they can expect to be blindsided someday when their best performers serve notice that they are leaving for another job. And in many cases, that someone leaves not only his or her business unit but also leaves the company for another organization. So the manager loses a talented person, and the company loses a talented person. What a shame.

Instead of ignoring people's desires to advance their careers, managers should become partners in exploring new opportunities. I happen to agree that employees are in fact responsible for their own careers. But this is not a good reason for a manager to sit on the sidelines. Instead, managers should see themselves as a kind of consultant or coach for their employees who want to consider career options.

What are the best ways to be a career coach to your employees? First, get folks to consider the big picture and the landscape of opportunity in your organization. Second, help folks understand what future roles might be right for them. Third, help folks imagine paths toward their career goals.

I'll comment on big pictures and landscapes here and then turn my attention to targeting the right roles and charting the right path to those roles in the next chapter.

Most of us tend to think of careers in terms of the roles we want. "I want to be a manager." "I want to be a senior accountant." "I want to be a marketing specialist." This is perfectly normal and understandable. However, I think this is not the most productive place to start a "What's next for me?" conversation. I think it is better to start with this big picture/landscape question.

What big problems here at our organization would you like to help solve? This question does a couple of things. First, it helps remind your employee of a simple truth: that the most valued employees in most organizations are the ones seen as solving the big problems. Honestly, anyone known in an organization for seriously contributing to the solutions of big problems is golden. I have known some people who have built their whole career by simply tackling their organization's big issues and letting which role they happen to be in just work itself out. Second, the question tends to reveal someone's professional passions and interests, a key component to uncovering potentially satisfying roles.

A manager and his or her employee can learn a great deal about satisfying career trajectories simply by asking this question first.

Career Moments and the Career Lattice

Once that big picture question has been asked and answered, I suggest the manager explore with his or her employee what I call "career moments." Career moments are those times in our careers when three things happen simultaneously:

1. You're doing something you are talented or skilled at.
2. You're doing something you are passionate about.
3. You're doing something that someone will pay you a fair salary or wage to do.

"… the most engaged employees are the ones who are also passionate about what they do."

Think about it. Isn't this what we all strive for in a career? Doing work that we are good at, that we like to do, and that someone will pay us for? Whenever I have spoken with folks about their careers and asked them what their favorite moments in those careers have been, these three conditions are almost always being met. This is why I call them "career moments."

Honestly, only the very lucky can look back on their careers and say they spent every moment in a "career moment." Most of us spend some portions of our careers doing things we are talented at and someone will pay us to do. Not a terrible arrangement. Your bills get paid. It puts food on the table. For many of us, our first jobs were like this. And for many reasons, a number of jobs throughout our careers are like this as well.

But the most engaged employees are the ones who are also passionate about what they do.

As a career coach, a manager can use this notion of "career moments" to help a staff member explore what future roles would be remarkably satisfying and which would be simply satisfactory. You can do this by helping people sort out what they are talented at, what they are passionate about, and what pay expectations they have. This is probably best understood by looking in on a "What's next for me?" conversation, which we will do in the next chapter.

Once staff members can begin to imagine jobs or roles that might provide them a career moment, the manager can also help them imagine the first step on the path to those roles. Many years ago the path to a new role was one direction: up. Anything other than "up" was considered career foolishness. This is no longer the case. Today career paths are made up of three kinds of moves: "up," "over," and "more." Sometimes, in the pursuit of a career moment, the best move will in fact be a job further up the organizational ladder. But sometimes the ultimate career goal requires a very different set of skills and experiences that can only be achieved by moving laterally or "over" in the organization. Today this is a quite acceptable career move. And because of the significant downsizing and flattening of many organizations, simply taking on more work in the current role can have the same impact as moving laterally—gaining new skills and experience.

Here is an example of the career progression of a friend of mine. As you see, if is full of ups, overs, and mores.

- credit analyst (first job)
- credit supervisor (up)
- customer operations manager (up)
- quality assurance manager (over)
- instructional designer/trainer (over)
- head of training administration (up)
- head of learning administration (more)
- head of talent management (up)
- vice president of HR (up)
- vice president of real estate (over)

So the career ladder has been replaced with a career lattice—a kind of jigsaw puzzle of career opportunity. And notice in this example how the career moved across different business disciplines: credit, quality, HR, and real estate. Different career trajectories based on a shifting definition of career moments. Most of us work a long time, and our work choices can reflect changing preferences and circumstances in our lives. So it should not be surprising to see careers move in something other than a straight line. This is why a manager as career coach can help.

In the "What's next for me?" conversation a manager can help someone clarify both what career moments might be and suggest the right next step (up/over/more) toward a career moment.

Example of a "What's Next for Me?" Conversation

Nancy: Steve, it has been a while since we talked about what might be next for you. Thought it would be a good thing to catch up.

Steve: Thanks, me too.

Nancy: This last year you began to add more consulting to your portfolio of work. You thought at the time it would be a good skill to match up with your training and development experiences. I have to say that when you found the time for it, the folks you have been working with were pretty happy. As I suspected, you seem to have some talent in consulting.

Steve: Thanks. Really, I find consulting on process improvement not unlike needs assessment work for training and development. I think I am using very similar muscles, so to speak. I am sure there is plenty more to learn about consulting. I still think it's a good skill set for me to continue to hone.

Nancy: Are you enjoying it?

Steve: Well, sometimes. It's new and something different. But I can tell already I prefer the training work.

Nancy: Why?

Steve: It's hard to see the impact I make when I am consulting on process improvement work. When I design training, I collaborate with others, but I feel like the design is mine. And when I facilitate a classroom, I feel I can see the impact I am having right there in the moment. With consulting I don't have the feeling of ownership or the immediate gratification.

Nancy: So you're not passionate about it?

Steve: No, not really. Don't get me wrong though. I want to continue to grow this skill. I think I need it if someday I want to run a large learning and development group. I see that kind of role needing a consulting competency. Do you agree?

Nancy: Yes. But if part of what you like about design work and being an instructor is some immediate gratification and singular ownership, I wonder about that larger role you're interested in. Larger roles often focus on longer-term issues. They typically are not a place of instant gratification. And ownership of anything in a senior role can be a bit of a mirage.

Steve: I understand. But I believe that if the larger job is focused on learning and development, my love for that work will outweigh some of that instant gratification.

Nancy: Maybe. In the meantime, if you are looking to expand the consulting experiences, we can do one of two things. Either I can add some more consulting to your current plate. Or we could talk about you transferring over to the quality management group in the next year where your entire plate can be consulting. Which sounds like a better path? I can tell you right now some of the biggest, highest profile issues in the bank involve the quality management group.

Commentary on the Conversation

In this conversation we see Nancy using the "career moment" framework to acknowledge Steve's talent at consulting and check in on his passion. Nancy explored why Steve was not passionate about consulting and even challenged his longer-term career goal suggesting that perhaps he has a misplaced sense of that more senior role as a potential career moment.

Nancy and Steve seemed to agree that while consulting itself was not creating a current career moment, continuing to expand these skills was important. Nancy then proceeded to offer up two options: more or over. "More" allowed for a more balanced portfolio of work; "over" offered a more singular focus on consulting. Nancy also suggested that perhaps the "over" option might provide an opportunity to address a high-profile issue in the bank. This offer and this insight give Steve the chance to consider how deeply he wants to hone his consulting skills.

"What's next for me?" conversations can often become awkward if the employee expresses unrealistic career goals. This often happens when employees have an unrealistic view of their talents and the talents required for the job they aspire to.

Steve: What I really would like is to be leader of the trust department someday.

Nancy: Really? I'm surprised. You don't have any banking experience or trust experience at all. True, you do work in a bank. But all of your experiences have been in HR here and before you came to us. Why the trust department and why the leader?

So Nancy is getting at Steve's motivation to explore such an unlikely career aspiration.

Steve: The more I work with that department, the more interesting I find their work. And since my long-term goal is a leadership position, it seems like a good goal.

It isn't Nancy's job to discourage Steve as much as it is to inform Steve of the requirements of employment in the trust department and the requirements of leading such a department. In this case employment in that department requires a business or finance degree (neither of which Steve has), a track record of success as a trust professional, and succession through at least three levels of bank management in order to arrive at the job he covets.

There are many different "career moments" waiting for all of us, depending on which professional tracks we pursue. A manager is wise to remind someone exploring a path littered with practical obstacles that there are other paths more easily taken that can yield great career moments. People are responsible for managing their own careers, so the final decisions are theirs. But managers can bring wisdom and perspective to career conversations that can help people be both aspirational and practical at the same time.

Some Final Thoughts

The six conversations are a framework designed to address what might be considered the most fundamental or basic activities a manager must pay attention to when managing people. The emphasis has been on "conversations," not processes. But as mentioned many times throughout the book, once great conversations have occurred, certain talent processes must be served.

I don't want to leave anyone who reads this thinking that the job of a manager is just about six conversations. There are tones of respect and fairness and other cultural issues that need attention. And as a manager grows proficient in these six conversations, techniques for addressing more sophisticated people issues, such as teamwork, conflict resolution, and change management, need to fold into the manager's portfolio of competencies.

Also, there is another dimension of the manager's role besides people management. That would be "process management." Most managers are responsible not only for the performance of their team but also for the performance of a handful of processes. I have known managers who are excellent with their people but clueless about the processes they oversee for the client's (external or internal) needs. These managers tend not to do very well. It would be like managing a team and only focusing on the offense, leaving the defense to chance. Anyone interested in being a successful manager must master process management as well as people management.

The techniques outlined in this book are necessary but not the totality of being a good manager. Sometimes a statement like that seems as if it diminishes the value of these conversations. On the contrary, I think the statement highlights the absolute value of these six conversations and the contribution they make to Drucker's challenge to managers: "to bring out the best in employees, strengthen their integrity, and train them to stand upright and strong."

So go have some good conversations. Your employees will be better for it. Your organization will be better for it. And so will you.

Recommended Reading

Much of what I have presented in this book has come from my experiences and those of hundreds of others who have shaped my view of managing. There have been some books that have also shaped my thinking. I would recommend each of these for anyone interested in digging deeper into the best practices of management.

For a great overview of the job of a manager, I would recommend:

Hill, Linda, and Kent Lineback. *Being the Boss*. Boston: Harvard Business Review Press, 2011.

The Peter Drucker quote at the beginning of the book was drawn from:

Drucker, Peter. *The Practice of Management*. New York: Harper Business, 2006.

For insight into what makes someone come up clutch in a difficult situation, I suggest:

Sullivan, Paul. *Clutch*. New York: Portfolio/Penguin, 2010.

For more insights into what motivates great performance, I would recommend:

Pink, Daniel. *Drive*. New York: Riverhead Books, 2009.

Thomas, Kenneth. *Intrinsic Motivation at Work*. San Francisco: Berrett-Koehler, 2000.

For suggestions on how to manage people smarter than us, I would recommend:

Goffee, Rob, and Gareth Jones. *Clever*. Boston: Harvard Business Press, 2009.

For more about the "brag, worry, wonder, bet" framework for giving feedback, you can read my book:

King, Steve. *Brag, Worry, Wonder, Bet.* Bloomington, IN: iUniverse, 2014.

About the Author

Steve King is the executive director of the Center for Professional and Executive Development at the University of Wisconsin's School of Business and president of the SDK Group, which specializes in helping organizations find solutions with their talent management challenges.

Steve is the retired senior vice president of human resources for Hewitt Associates, a global human resource consulting and outsourcing firm. He has also served as the head of global talent management for Baxter Healthcare, faculty leader for the Bank of Montreal's Institute for Learning in Toronto, and vice president of management and professional development for Harris Bank in Chicago.

In Steve's early career years, he was an instructor and curriculum designer for the Wisconsin Vocational and Technical System.

Steve lives in Chicago, splitting his time between Madison, Wisconsin, and the Chicagoland area.

Anyone interested in contacting Steve or ordering this book can go to Steve's website … www.bragworrywonderbet.com

CPSIA information can be obtained
at www.ICGtesting.com
Printed in the USA
FFOW05n1746181116